MACCLESFIELD

◆ *in Pictures & Poems* ◆

DOROTHY BENTLEY SMITH

Published by Sigma Leisure - an imprint of
Sigma Press, 1 South Oak Lane, Wilmslow, Cheshire SK9 6AR, England.

British Library Cataloguing in Publication Data: A CIP record for this book is available from the British Library.

ISBN: 1-85058-550-4

Typesetting, design and printing by: MFP Design and Print

Cover photograph: Late 18th Century Silk Mill, Park Green, Macclesfield

CONTENTS

This is where it all began..... 1
South Park 2
Folk Tales..9
Park Green & Park Lane 12
Macclesfield Market 18
108 Steps 20
The Question (Sunderland St.) 22
Public Houses 24
Macclesfield Canal 28
For Sale (Lord St.) 29
Christ Church 32
Market Cross 38
The Silk Road 39
Le Roi Soleil 43
Comment..46
Hovis Factory 48
A Favourite Pastime (Bowling).....................................50
Heads but no Tales 53
Bollin Valley..56
1745 - A Page in Macclesfield History 58
A Touch of Italy (Shaw St.) 63
Venetian Window 64
The Totem Pole (Croker Hill)..68
Nonsery Rhymes 70
Modern Macclesfield 80
Our New Library 86
A Sign of Old Age (Chestergate) 88
The Doll's House (Chestergate) 90
Waters Green 94
A Thought 97
The Saucer 98
V.E. Day Remembered 101
A Ramble Through Macclesfield....................................102

ILLUSTRATIONS

Macclesfield Forest from Tegg's Nose 1

View from South Park 3

Bandstand - South Park 6

Ducks on South Park lake 7

Avenue of trees - South Park 8

Myths & Legends 11

Former silk mill - Park Green 12

Demolition on Park Lane 13

Twelve Apostles - Park Lane 15

Springtime blossoms - Park Lane 17

Late Victorian market - Macclesfield 18

108 Steps 20

Snooker Hall - Sunderland St. 22

Lord Byron public house 24

Bridgewater Arms public house 26

Macclesfield canal from Buxton Road 28

Houses for sale on Lord St. 30

Views of Christ Church 33

Bust of John Wesley 35

Font and organ Christ Church 35

Christ Church viewed from Park Lane roundabout 37

Market Cross 38

Map of Old Silk Road 41

New Silk Road - Macclesfield 42

St. Michael's gates 44

Graffiti pedestrian walkway Park Lane 47

Hovis Mill 48

Pack Horse bowling green, Westminster Rd. 51

West Park bowling green 51

Heads over doorways - Newton St. 53

Heads on old G.P.O. Castle St. 54

Horse's head on the Nag's Head public house 55

River Bollin from a bridge in Bollin Valley 57

Jordangate 59

St. Michael's Church 1850 59

Market Place Macclesfield 61

Cumberland House Jordangate 62

Rear of house on Shaw St. 63

Venetian windows 65

Mast on Croker Hill looking towards Sutton 69

Boulder in West Park...70
Houses with garrets on Paradise St. 71
Christmas crib in the Market Place 72
Parish Church of St. Michael's & All Saints 73
New extension of the Town Hall 75
Festivals House on Park Lane 76
Nicholas Winterton M.P. 77
Aviary in West Park 78
Two 'sleeping beauties' West Park 79
Buildings Churchill Way 80
Regency Mill - Chester Rd. roundabout 81
Houses on Brown St. 82
Edwardian fireplace 83
Obelisk in old Dissenting graveyard - Roe St. 84
Original 1823 entrance to the Town Hall 85
New library on Jordangate 86
A doorway on Chestergate 88
Drawing of 18th century doorway on Chestergate....................89
Charles Roe house on Chestergate...92
Waters Green c. 1810 95
Saucer - Roe St. Sunday School commemorative 99
White Swan public house Rodney St. 101
View behind Town Hall & Parish Church 102
Trees in West Park...111
Window depicting Queen Eleanor - Parish Church 112
The Savage Chapel - Parish Church 113
Drawing of the old Grammar School 114
Original entrance of Parish Church 115
Old Bank Building King Edward St. 116
Portrait of John Stafford 117
Portrait of Charles Roe 118
The Angel Inn in the Market Place c. 1940............................119
Portrait of Edward Hawkins 120
West Park Museum 121
Gawsworth Hall 122
Grave of 'Lord Flame' Gawsworth 123
Part of former chapel Park Lane roundabout 124
Houses on Park Lane..125
View from the rear of the Parish Church 126

Dedication

To Muriel Walker, who introduced many Maxonians to poetry and was a co-founder of the Macclesfield Music and Drama Festival.

Acknowledgements

My sincere thanks to a good friend Eileen Talbot for correcting any mistakes, and to my daughter, Victoria, for her excellent illustrations on pages 11, 41, 89 and 114. Also to the Macclesfield Community News for allowing reproduction of photographs on pages 69 and 77 and to Mrs. Norna Dakin for allowing me to copy prints in her possession for the illustrations on pages 18, 59 and 95.

Portraits

Edward Hawkins, page 120, is reproduced by kind permission of the owner.

Charles Roe, page 118, is reproduced by kind permission of the Churches Conservation Trust.

John Stafford, page 117: every endeavour has been made to trace the owner of the original portrait, but without success.

DEAR READER,

As an only child growing up during the last war life could be lonely at times; there weren't many children around. Everything seemed dark and dreary and there was always the uncertainty of how long things would remain that way. I escaped into a wonderful world of books, in particular learning to love and appreciate poetry.

I was fascinated by the way in which words could be manipulated to form rhythms and yet, at the same time, convey to the reader a deeper understanding of what was in the composer's mind. I began to experiment, it was great fun finding words that rhymed and then working out ideas to fit - better than a crossword puzzle.

My favourite poem was, and still is, Wordsworth's "Composed Upon Westminster Bridge", written almost 200 years ago. When I eventually stood upon Westminster Bridge early one Sunday morning on a glorious summer's day, the poignancy of that beautiful poem overwhelmed me; it was just as relevant then as the day it had been written.

I don't profess to be another Wordsworth, far from it, but living in Macclesfield for almost 30 years has inspired me to think in verse on many occasions.

We all see Macclesfield in many different ways and I hope you will enjoy experiencing my Macclesfield.

Dorothy Bentley Smith.

What is a poem?
What does it do?
Will it bring joy to me and you?

It's a story in rhyme, a thought set out better,
More interesting far than a boring old letter!

A view from Tegg's Nose looking
east towards what remains of
Macclesfield Forest.

This is where it all began a thousand years ago, or more,

The wooded hillsides overrun with rabbits, wolves and boar.

...a face in every summer's sky?

THOUGHTS ON A VIEW FROM SOUTH PARK

Can I really see a face in every summer's sky?

Or is it all a pantomime as clouds drift idly by?

The vivid glow of sunset, sending orange bands of light

Across a verge of grey-black space, illuminating night

And conjuring up great mountain peaks with icy silhouettes,

Which melt away before my eyes into hazy coronets.

When autumn brings a different scene it makes me want to cry,

Remembering many tragedies beneath its murky sky.

No time for forming pictures as each day turns into night;

The mass of swirling thick black clouds obliterate the flight

Of birds migrating to the sun, as if trapped within its nets,

And curious heavens descend at dawn, expressing their regrets.

2

Looking north towards Macclesfield.
An early evening view from the
highest point on the miniature golf
course in South Park.

The crisp bright clouds of springtime make the showers, which seem a lie,

A happy cheery beaming farce to set the world awry.

For after winter's darkness I looked for hope and light

By raising eyes up to the heavens to see a welcome sight

But foolishness takes over joy, for as the red sun sets

We all can dream of bright blue skies, as happiness expects.

WHAT AM I?

Poor, old majestic thing,

How have you managed to survive this long

and not become a glorious heap of rubble?

There is talk of restoration,

But will you be as useful then as you are now,

when goal posts are so few and far between?

You still perform your task.

You know you're there to entertain, and whatever

mask you wear does not obliterate your purposefulness.

The audience might change,

But it too lingers on. The chairs are gone

Yet still the seats remain, convenient grassy pews.

Conductors came and went,

As instruments thumped long and hard, and notes,

resounding through the air, were hurled across the park.

And who conducts this time?

A skinny youth with baggy pants and sloppy coat,

who dashes to and fro, exhorting all to shout and bawl.

He loves the centre stage.

A great performance, by the sound of claps and cheers and

clanking cans thrown wild across your boards.

And do you really care?

The remnants of your former crowds pass by and

criticize, or turn away pretending you're not there.

Please turn the page . . .

The bandstand in South Park,
Macclesfield.

"Please turn the page", you beg,

"Now see me as I really am, with bushes for my hair,

a shape to shelter and console".

"When shadows fall at dusk"

"And echoes from a distant place float gently past the lake,

my ducks will pay their nightly call."

"Their quacks are harmony",

"I love them well those constant faithful friends, for most of

all their loyalty remains."

creep to the lake...

Ducks on the lake in South Park, Macclesfield. A favourite place for children who love to throw bread to the birds.

THE DUCKS

Creep to the lake — it's raining,

Creep to the lake and see

How many ducks are waiting

To be fed by you and me.

7

peace...

The avenue of trees South Park,
Macclesfield.

PEACE — a rare commodity,

Often confused with tranquil happiness.

A harmony in nature which pleases man.

Serenity with gentle sounds, as rustling leaves

Enshroud my path down to the lake,

And leave me with a momentary mind of PEACE.

Ancient myths and legends are fascinating things,

Witches and their covens, armoured knights and kings.

Stories handed down to help us pass the time,

Exaggerated happenings remembered best in rhyme.

Alderley has spectres inhabiting its caves,

Attracting groups of weirdos intent on having raves,

But in the summer sunlight or in the autumn rain

The prehistoric creatures run to earth again.

A bowl of Roman coinage, an exciting recent find

Hints of Roman soldiers, or a legion left behind

To find the Edge's treasures, its coffers to maintain,

For tributes to the Emperor were not their only aim.

Congleton is Bear Town, so the story goes.

When one day the bear died a murmuring arose.

"Our bear we want replacing, but how can this be done?"

"We'll sell our Holy Bible, a bear is much more fun!"

But in the nineteenth century when poverty arrived,

There was no Council Bible, of that they'd been deprived,

'Cos earlier generations had thought they'd chosen well,

But with no bear or Bible, the place seemed just like Hell.

Sophisticated Knutsford with Tatton Park supreme,

Can boast of Mrs. Gaskell and streets petite and clean,

Of hostelries and tea rooms and everything that's nice,

Antiques and lovely furniture — but only at a price!

And charming little Prestbury was Mother to our town

For Macclesfield was tiny, now the role's reversed around.

No petrol pumps or gaudy shops can spoil the former's pride,

No rubbish dumps or dirty paths the Council needs to hide.

This pretty little village serves a band elite,

Who much prefer its quaintness and its one and only street.

Let those who want consider a town's a better place,

Who'd think we all are creatures of the same old human race?

The story says in Silk Town one day a horse and cart

Pulled up the hill of Mill Street; its driver gave a start,

For from behind his waggon a barrel rolled and fell

And out of it poured treacle like a rising sticky well.

Yet Treacle Town's exciting, its history is long.

With silk brought to perfection where did it all go wrong?

Where went the dedication when the man-made fibre trend

Saw skills of generations come to a 'sticky end'?

hoping to improve...

Conservation — Preservation

Busy bees in Council hives,

Restoration — Perpetuation,

Hoping to improve our lives.

Former Silk Mill, Park Green

Demolition of houses on Park Lane

Obliteration — Eradication

Blanking out the face of time.

Elimination — extermination

A new look vote or just a crime?

...just a crime?

...Edwardian built and planned

THE TWELVE APOSTLES

With red bricks shining in the sun,

Austere and proud they stand,

Three stories high and chimneys tall,

Edwardian built and planned.

Their names are not of holy note,

As Peter, James and John,

Still they command respectful fame

From those who pass along.

The gardens unpretentious, small,

With privet hedging round

Have paths which sweep to large stone steps,

Built high above the ground.

The doors are large and stout and strong,

Two columns standing guard,

And half moon windows facing south

Help brighten each facade.

The bays of stone suggest their views

Of height and distant sights

A park with bowling green and trees

Where setting sun delights.

The row known as the Twelve Apostles, Park Lane.

Each attic window neat and small

Belies its inner space

And sashes still remain intact

Conserving form and grace.

These upper stores are so arranged

That two by two they plot

A pattern overall, which runs

The whole length of the block.

Although the rooms are Georgian style,

Deep skirtings, cornice, tiles,

Their warmth and power instil in all

A presence that beguiles

15

AGI'S TREE

A cup of tea, a comfy chair
And out of my window I love to stare
Impelled and drawn to the tree — Agi's tree.

Six years ago, or was it five?,
My Persian pussy was still alive,
She loved to roam everywhere — anywhere.

A loyal friend, a mouser great
Till an ageing heart had sealed her fate,
And eighteen years seemed like none — she was gone.

"Remember me — keep me alive",
I had promised her and I must contrive,
To fulfil the wish, I would try — really try.

A tiny grave, a garden small,
Lots of traffic passing beyond the wall,
She must live through something good — really good.

A special rose, a flowering bush?,
But my son said "No its not good enough",
And a tree he found, "That's like me"- she'd agree.

Red berries bright, dull days decry,
When the springtime blossoms delight the eye,
Then the world admires and loves — really loves.

Springtime blossom in Park Lane.

delight the eye...

The market's got a problem...

Late Victorian view of Macclesfield market.

MACCLESFIELD MARKET

The market's got a problem, it has to move again.

How often have those market stalls face wind and snow and rain?

For centuries they've managed, survived the summer heat,

Have moved and moved from site to site, but now they face defeat.

For centuries the people had flocked into the town.

To buy the horses, cattle, beer for which it had renown.

Then modern times took over, and cars replaced the feet

Old fashioned ways and farming types becoming obsolete.

But Market Place and Waters soon saw another change,

With handbag stalls and birthday cards and goods throughout the range.

Soon fruit and veg. declining and fish completely gone,

Drew smaller crowds and folks forgot when shopping was such fun!

108 steps

20

108 STEPS

"Are there really 108 steps?" the little boy asked his brother

"I don't know".

"Are there really 108 steps?" the little boy asked his mother

"I suppose so".

"Are there really 108 steps?" the little boy asked his friend

"I think there are".

"Well I've been up and down and counted them — and its driven

me round the bend!

only they can answer . . .

The gateway to Sunderland Street Chapel, built 1779, extended 1799,
where John Wesley preached. Today the chapel is a snooker hall.

THE QUESTION

Every generation thinks it knows it all,

Every generation builds its own brick wall.

Does it think it's better to keep the enemy out?

Or is it locking out good friends who could help to quell its rout?

Every human being knows what he most desires,

Every human being helps light his own bonfires.

But will they reap destruction, or use the warmth and light

To heal the plight of poorer souls who are starving in the night?

Only they can answer; then will it be too late?

Only they can answer by putting in a gate.

That way there is an option to open or to close,

To half let in or half let out for whatever they suppose.

...memory lingers on

Lord Byron public house on Chapel Street.

THE LORD BYRON

What funny face is on that sign,

I wonder if Lord Byron cares.

Somehow I doubt that he'd be pleased,

The elegance hardly compares.

His verses dealt with calm and grace

And beauty natural and divine,

Not pulling pints or throwing darts,

Though common interest could be wine!

What's in a name? — a mighty lot.

At least his memory lingers on.

We old ones might recall his works,

You young ones thankful that he's gone.

To glide along . . .

The Bridgewater Arms public house Buxton Road.

THE BRIDGEWATER ARMS
(In memory of the Duke of Bridgewater)

What nonsense made someone decide to name this pub in such a way?

This gentleman caused grief and strife to honest men along the way.

Although the Macclesfield canal is through the door, across the street,

It's thanks to him that early plans were over-ruled and met defeat.

When sheer desire to take command of all the waterways in sight

Caused him great loans, fiancées left, and filled his heart with hate and spite.

His Excellence decided then a gondola was just the thing

To glide along his 'Grand Canal', and now commercials mimic him!

Macclesfield Canal from the bridge on Buxton Road.

THE MACCLESFIELD CANAL

The calm of Sunday morning invites a tranquil scene,

Barges at their moorings, no humans intervene,

There's just a strip of water, (the ducks have put to flight),

And church tower in the distance that makes the world seem right.

FOR SALE

It's spring and everywhere the signs hang out 'FOR SALE',

But what makes people want to move just then?

They think, perhaps, that none will trudge through wind and gale,

To look around their house or precious little den.

So winter months see unresolved the problems of a few,

And summer months see crowds of boards all begging folks to view.

'FOR SALE', a simple sign compelling one to see

What lies within those walls or through that door.

To view at certain times, will cause to some degree,

An inconvenience or a visit to ignore.

Yet still a curious few will call to judge how others live,

A spurious way to pass their time, not easy to forgive.

And those with genuine thoughts who want to look around,

May find themselves bewildered by the choice,

But price must be a reckoning to keep in mind,

With hopes that bargains can be made with solemn voice.

The hunt is on, the search begins, enthusiasm flows,

The tireless treks, the nightly jaunts keep viewers on their toes.

a broken home...

Houses for sale on Lord Street, Macclesfield, during the summer of 1995.

But when, as autumn nights turn chilly and grow dark,

The sellers think it's not the time to move,

Dilemmas spread and then perhaps a chance remark

Brings gloom and despond near, an action to reprove.

And yet next year the lucky ones will see their signs marked 'SOLD',

As those who braved the winter months caught bargains with their colds.

The words 'SUBJECT TO CONTRACT' can have a hollow ring

And cause some anxious moments for a while.

A survey done can oft reveal some nasty thing,

A cellar full of damp, dry rot — that dread profile.

Though many, anxious to conceal, will paint and cover well,

An expert eye detects the faults, one wishes it to hell!

Well done you privileged few who buy and sell with ease,

Your reasons seem superfluous to the cause,

But then those Agents eager to improve their fees,

Ignore the human toll, bogged down by ancient laws.

A broken home, a bankrupt soul, a time to repossess,

Those signs present the gaudy face of failure or success.

CHARLIE'S CHURCH

Whichever way one looks to town it's there,

Charlie's church — a crenellated tower in the air.

Its height ensures that anyone who wants to know,

Can tell the time or merely find the way to go.

Some people said that vanity and pride

Built it so — misunderstood and jealous they had lied.

A youthful wish, a promise kept by Mr. Roe

And in their hearts how could they say it wasn't so!

When as a child his parents died he found

Life is hard — but totally undaunted he looked round.

The button trade of linen, hair and silk he chose,

And from this work, with effort great, a silk mill rose.

Nor did he think to stop and face despair,

Fortunes fell — for always wisdom taught him to take care,

And copper mines, with smelting mills from which brass rolled

Brought to the firm in time much wealth like 'pots of gold'.

But with his wealth he did not plan to build

Spacious halls — or mansion house inspiring to behold.

The teeming town of Macclesfield would grow and grow,

With churchyard full and crowded pews, where could folk go

views of Christ Church...

From Crompton Road

From Newton Street

Two views from South Park.

John Wesley came to town each year to preach

Sermons long — a splendid opportunity to teach.

Though Church of England minister he fought the foe

Of lethargy and apathy, but work was slow.

His audience grew larger every year

Out of love — his methods drew a gathering to hear.

And everyone who listened felt inspired to sing,

But Wesley found that not for him did church bells ring.

So Charles observed, "What did the people want,

Happy souls?" — "a chance to bring their children to the font?"

Five generations principles he sought to keep,

Respect for King and bishops due, a Church complete.

He wanted most a place for one and all,

Rich and poor — a ministry in waiting for his son.

An illness made him think and soon his plans took shape,

But skilful work controversy could not escape.

In summer heat the work was hurried on,

Walls grew tall — the body and the church became as one.

When, as the organ opened, music filled the air,

With many choirs, musicians famed and Handel's flair.

Rare late eighteenth-century miniature bust of John Wesley. Probably made shortly after his death in 1791.

18th century marble font — Christ Church

Christ Church organ — built eighteenth, but extensively restored in the nineteenth century.

At last his life's ambitions seemed complete,

Almost so — but Consecration proved another feat;

For as St. Michael's minister objected so,

The Bishop hesitated, but soon had to go.

Yet all was well, new Bishop Beilby came,

As Charles knew — a man of deep sound principles and fame.

The arguments raged long and hard, but not too slow

For Beilby was a copper partner's son-in-law!

The tower was added in the following year,

Seventy six — but two years on hysteria and fear

Swept through the church, as earthquake struck and people ran,

The shudder passed, the tower stood tall, its life began.

Though Wesley came and preached one Eastertime,

By request — the Reverend Simpson being in his prime,

Enthusiasm overtook, but soon he knew

John Wesley preaching there was not the thing to do.

So Wesley left and would not reappear

In that church — till after Charles Roe's death (he did adhere),

But then the niece of Mr. Roe, Miss Hester Anne,

Devised a scheme and stubbornly put forth her plan.

A Methodist at heart she helped create

A new faith — a chapel small where those could congregate

Who felt that Wesley should be heard, and then Charles knew

His hopes were dashed for reconciling Hester's crew.

Son Robert joined the Methodists one day,

Hester won — though Charles did plead, prevaricate and pray.

Till finally he died a broken hearted man,

Through actions of that foolish child, Miss Hester Anne.

Two large black horses dressed with mourning drapes,

Plodded on — the hearse formidable with black silk tapes,

And coffin laid to rest within the family vault,

His life had proved this clever man was earth's good salt.

Looking along Churchill Way towards Christ Church, from the Park Lane roundabout.

Remains of the old market cross outside the Parish Church of St. Michael's, Macclesfield.

TALKING CROSS PURPOSES

We had a market cross,

Now the cross has lost its cross,

So how can we get across,

Without tourists getting cross,

The fact that our market cross

Really is, at least was, a genuine cross?

crossed deserts, rivers, ...

THE SILK ROAD

Images that spring to mind of caravans and winding trails,

Suggestions too of perfumed groves, exotic lives and merchants great,

Stories for a thousand nights from tellers of Arabian tales,

Mysteries to hold us fast; how do these things to us relate?

We see a busy market place where traffic squeezes through each day,

And vehicles travelling north to south or south to north, divert aside,

But still they thunder on apace, then grind to halts on Churchill Way,

Disgorging fumes and clouds of smoke, which most of us cannot abide.

"A bypass really must be built", went out the cry in forty seven,

But forty long more years it took before the plans were underway,

A period of chaos came, re-routing, digs and sewers driven,

And now we have a half made road that leads "from where to where?" we say.

The Silk Road begs us to recall its namesake lost in desert sands,

But our few miles can hardly count, five thousand went before, we know,

Crossed deserts, rivers, mountains, plains and borders of so many lands,

Bleak foothills of Eurasian steppes, midst sunshine, thunder, rain and snow.

...mountains, plains and borders of so many lands

In the west was Antioch where travellers gathered to proceed,

For safety was their main concern, with camels by the hundred bidden,

Experienced guides and masters hired armed escorts 'cording to their needs,

And horses packed with merchandise, were led along but never ridden.

Deserts, awesome to behold, had sandstorms dashing hopes with fright,

Through Tarim, dunes three hundred feet, red suffocating shifting sands,

Caused sounds like goblins calling out to fearful travellers lost at night,

With wailing winds that led astray to capture by marauding bands.

So different routes at different times were used in order to avoid

The dangers, relayed back and forth along this never-ending trail,

The want of water, food and friends sometimes saw spirits near destroyed,

But walled oases offered hope and helped the silk routes to prevail.

The much awaited caravan, that slowly snaked its way along,

On seeing skirts of yellow sands embraced the valley of the Wei.

Here China's Wall reached furthest out to shelter and protect the throng,

With customs paid, they thankful trod the long Imperial Highway.

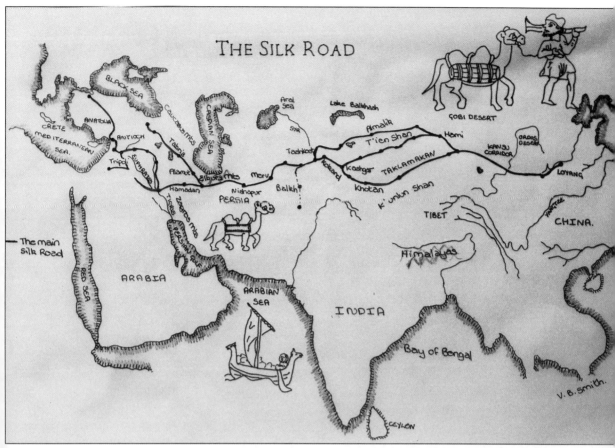

THE SILK ROAD

Map of The Silk Road stretching from
the Mediterranean Sea to the
furthest reaches of Northern China.

The journey's end was now in sight, LOYANG a city great and rich,

Where markets sold in each bazaar a specialised commodity,

There Western merchants sold their goods, no longer needing tents to pitch,

And in return they loaded up with iron, silks, new drugs and tea.

When Marco Polo paved the way for others to pursue their trades,

It was the thirteenth century, then Mongols sought to keep control.

Encouragement of Western ways saw no support for pirates' raids,

And Kublai Khan with Buddhist faith cast far his powers beyond the Wall.

Along the road, from time to time, the armies of great conquerors surged.

Attila's hordes swept far and wide inflicting terror as they swarmed,

But Alexander claimed the right for him the barbarous East to purge,

Let them despise, they will regret that Greek intelligence was scorned.

Sad when the silk road faded fast, as European navies grew,

Its threads had arced across the land, now ships began to strengthen routes,

No more the need to skirt the hills, the Iranian plateau horrors knew,

The 'roof top of the world' grew cold without the sound of merchants' boots.

Our road is trampled every day, but mostly traffic rolls along,

Yet commerce thrives as horsepower pulls the modern 'caravans' uphill,

Oases are a distant dream, no goblins sing a nightly song,

Though Macclesfield can hear the sound 'Silk Heritage' remains here still.

The Silk Road, Macclesfield.

sun rules all...

LE ROI SOLEIL

Cushion covers, curtain rails,

Everywhere the sun prevails.

Peering out from many frames,

Podgy face with hair of flames.

This new celestial body cult,

Aims to bring a swift result;

Boosting sales of household goods,

Brightening decor's tasting buds.

Unobserved this emblem reigns,

Same podgy face and wavy flames,

Staring 'cross the Market Place,

Accompanied by a form of Grace.

No moon or stars or planets there,

Just one small angel treading air.

This sun has held divinely court,

Keeping just its one consort.

Note: The sun in splendour was a badge of the House of Tudor. It had previously been used by Richard II, and in one instance a shield of his arms carries angels in attendance!

Wrought iron work over the gates leading to the parish church of St. Michael and All Angels, Macclesfield.

No Aztecs here or gods of fire

Consuming townfolks with desire.

We'll find it's just a French connection

Inspired the modern resurrection.

For Louis, King of France, ruled all

With radiance from within his soul.

Devotion to the heavenly star

Sent brilliant tales to places far.

THE SUN RULES ALL — became the theme,

The palace of Versailles the scene,

Where courtiers radiated too,

Ambassadors and faces new.

Abroad it was a new design

Symbolic of a great Divine.

So let's forgive the Georgian builder

Whose gates our modern eyes bewilder.

COMMENT

(On graffiti sprayed on the walls of a pedestrian subway close by the working silk museum)

WHAT DOES THIS MEAN?

A prehistoric painting in a cave makes far more sense.

THESE SYMBOLS PROVE

Our species dims as brains grow strangely muddled and more dense.

SOON WE'LL RETURN

To throwing rocks with howls and snarls — an animal pretence.

THOUGH CREATURES ALL

The animals have codes of careful conduct. — What's our defence?

46

NO COMMENT

The former Hovis Factory as seen from
the canal bridge on Buxton Road, with
the Macclesfield Marina in the
background.

A MACCLESFIELD FAVOURITE

*H*igh up on the small hillside of the Old Common

  *O*verlooking the picturesque Macclesfield Canal,

    *V*ying for its place in the Tourist Information,

      *I*s an old established name of every shopping mall.

        *S*uccess brought with it takeover and ultimate demise.

        *B*read made with a secret and special recipe.

      *R*emaining still a favourite, for many realize

    *E*xcellence and quality suit all the family.

  *A*nd now the building of its 'birth' is anxiously preserved,

*D*oes letting as a block of flats or business mean conserved?

a subtle game...

A FAVOURITE PASTIME

When Francis Drake supposedly remained to finish off his game of bowls,

Although the great Armada came with flags unfurled and hopes of winds and tides,

His action, though defiant, proved this game in favour, teaching skilled controls,

A pastime for an Englishman on English greens, where everyone contrives

To prove that playing last can have its gain of benefits and rich rewards,

A subtle game in which contenders use an eye that's true and judgment keen,

And one which individuals can play in partnerships or on their own,

A pastime linking centuries of sport in ruthless chase to reign supreme.

A lone bowler practising on the Pack Horse Club bowling green, Westminster Road.

Bowlers in West Park.

In Macclesfield some people of the town already knew this game of bowls

When Mayor and Aldermen proposed to set a green out on the Common side.

Three hundred years ago the terraces were neatly laid in grassy rows,

New players soon took up the game with rules and regulations to abide.

The bowling green became the leisure centre of those long lost early days,

With dancing, cards to entertain within pavilions, tea rooms or hotels.

And still today enthusiasm stays, for in our coolish summer climes,

In autumn rain or springtime mists one great Maxonian pastime still excels.

...this game of bowls

Two of the three houses at the northern end of Newton Street having heads over the doorways.

HEADS BUT NO TALES

Some considerable time ago, having moved house,

I was walking in a hurry to town

When I happened to see something which surprised me.

Three unusual brilliant heads, staring me down,

They were fixed on three doorways up high,

And I wanted to know who had designed this trio.

One looked like a man, one like Pan; the young girl was 'now',

Their expressions were real and concerned.

But of whom could I ask, "Of which modeller's task?"

53

As I stood in the G.P.O. waiting my turn,

My eyes wandered to windows across,

When I happened to see something which intrigued me.

Three unusual stone-carved heads, looking quite grand,

And the lion in the middle kept guard.

But I wanted to know why they were designed so.

Once again there were two like gods, over windows,

But the lion was the one for the door,

And I felt quite amused that no more had been used.

Former Post Office building on Castle Street now the Head Office of The Cheshire Building Society.

The horse's head over the doorway to the public house 'The Nag's Head' on Waters Green.

Now I've started to search for more, finding just one,

But its purpose is obvious to see;

It's the head of a horse — that's 'THE NAG'S HEAD' of course!

BOLLIN VALLEY

Quiet flows the Bollin on a summer's day,

Whilst overhead electric cables buzz and hum,

And bright yellow butterflies with such display,

Flutter round from bush to bush and look handsome.

Close by within a small and reedy pond,

The tadpoles wriggle fast, then quickly hide,

As convenient clumps of mossy reed respond

And act as soft warm beds in which to glide.

Yet vacant still the picnic tables strangely stand,

Though children splash around downstream and shout,

And buttercups crowd in to satisfy demand,

Which helps create a nature trail for those without.

The River Bollin from a bridge along the
Bollin Valley Nature Trail: a project sponsored by
Macclesfield Borough Council amongst others.

1745 — A PAGE IN MACCLESFIELD HISTORY

Tr-amp, tr-amp, tr-amp, tr-amp, the dreaded sound was heard,

Marching feet on Jordangate and quickly spread the word.

From Manchester the rebels came, had hastened on at speed,

Passed swiftly through old Stockport Town as the Prince himself decreed.

The time was almost ten o'clock, the Sunday morning fine,

When the Mayoress, breakfasting in style, had invited in to dine

A young Dragoon, an officer, who with his twenty men

Had arrived in town the previous night, intent on "digging in".

His words were reassuring, Madame Frances felt relief,

"Never fear Ma'am — we'll protect you", then, like a disturbed thief,

As word arrived, down went his dish and with all speed he left,

With Madame close in hot pursuit before she was bereft.

"The good Folks" in St. Michael's church the service left behind,

As they surged across the Market Place confused with panic blind.

A regiment of Horse rode in, Lord Elcho's to command,

And quarters for his troops he sought as he issued each demand.

Jordangate today, which in the eighteenth century
continued to the corner of Chestergate.

St. Michael's Church 1850, as it had stood since the extensive
alterations of 1740 when the spire had been removed.

That day the Duke of Perth appeared, with Colonels leading on

Each regiment in Highland Dress, before a dismayed throng;

And soon the Prince himself arrived on foot, but walking well,

Blue waistcoat edged with silver trim, consternation to dispel.

In haste, the town's folk dreading all, a peal of bells contrived,

But the team had quickly disappeared and only four arrived.

For fear of insults and much worse an effort great was made,

Yet the peal of bells was backward rung to the shambling rear parade!

With bagpipes loud instead of drums the show passed for some time,

Before a gathering at the Cross with a Mayor no more sublime,

And Aldermen in abject shock as Proclamation read,

Declared the Prince's father King, before crowd in silent dread.

Ten thousand troops were said to come, but only six arrived,

Concealment of their numbers, arms and routes had been contrived.

The Prince slept in Sir Peter's house (of tax collection fame),

These quarters, renamed Holyrood, the Grammar School became.

Market Place today with the remains of the Cross on the right. The Cross originally stood much closer to the site of the building on the right, then occupied by the Angel Inn. At the time of Bonnie Prince Charlie's visit the Market Place was only half the size it is now.

During those December days so many things took place,

Upsets, thieving, quarrelling, a 'cauldron' of disgrace.

As history tells, the army left to march on Derby Town,

The Bonnie Prince convinced he'd reach fair London and the Crown.

But Fate had still its hand to play as worn out, disarrayed

Commanders of the Highland throng their doubtful thoughts conveyed.

Meanwhile the Duke of Cumberland with army, from the south

Instilled alarm, as messages were relayed mouth to mouth.

So angry Prince retreated fast across the Derby hills,

And stragglers reaching Macclesfield revenged for all their ills.

Yet soon His Grace the Duke arrived and stayed on Jordangate,

The Stafford house, to his delight, convenient for his wait.

For three full nights he rested well, until the Friday came,

The thirteenth of December saw the Duke on horse again

With H.M. Forces. At their head he rode off north to quell

And conquer on Culloden Field his father's arch rival.

Holyrood has long since gone but Cumberland remains,

A name of pride that lingers on, which owners have retained.

A building of historic worth with plaque for all to see,

A friendly, happy, living place — a doctor's surgery.

Cumberland House on Jordangate with the plaque clearly visible.

Rear of a house on
Shaw Street.

A TOUCH OF ITALY

In a quiet corner near the heart of town

An Italian sense of style is on display.

Delightful Doric columns to balconies reach down

Where peaceful thoughts help pass the time of day.

In this very English and busy market sphere

It's scenes like this that interest and beguile,

For regimented houses create no atmosphere,

Yet elegance gives pleasure that's worthwhile.

Venetian window
Cumberland House,
Jordangate.

THE VENETIAN WINDOW

You must agree my grandeur is supreme,

I am a prince amongst the windows of this town.

My Doric styled pilasters painted cream

Support the patterned mouldings of my crown.

Venetian window above the doorway to the Doctor's Surgery, Sunderland Street.

My cousin almost ranks with me in pride,

His two tier ostentatious columns form

A doorway 'neath a window, not so wide

As to present a gracious structure as my own.

Venetian window
Charles Roe House
mid 1740s.

Some other windows of our form look grand,

We happily concede their early birth,

But mimicry soon took an upper hand

Demeaning our artistic style and worth.

I ask you now to ponder and observe

The shape and style and sizes of our group,

For windows are important to the world

And looking through you often overlook.

Macclesfield Arms Hotel built early nineteenth century showing the Venetian windows are only token in style.

Property on Park Green: on the right of the picture very little effort has been made to construct this Venetian styled window. Again nineteenth century.

THE TOTEM POLE

Neatly reminiscent of a totem pole, the telecommunications mast on Croker Hill

Adds its own distinctive signature to a landscape of otherwise bland yet undulating beauty.

This consequential link in a system of important human contact, imposes its own will

In an unobtrusive but imperative network, to relay messages to each independent community.

A totem is symbolic of a particular tribe of people, found mostly in America,

Derived from their own special connection with a plant, animal or other object from which they

claim descent.

Found also amongst the aboriginal tribes of Australia and Africa,

Its representative and visual form is carved carefully upon a pole in complement.

The mast on Croker Hill as seen beyond Sutton village.

A clear day keeps in sight this modern reassuring work of art near Macclesfield,

But clouds and rain can stir up mists to hide its constant presence from our view.

That it functions well is thanks to many skilled attendants from quite far-a-field,

Who, though not exactly worshipping at its shrine, its many individualistic parts renew.

...to relay messages

NONSERY RHYMES

A boulder, a stone, a large piece of rock, a mystery.

An object, a thing, a "call me what you will" of history.

The large boulder in West Park said
to have been transported to the area
originally by a glacier.

Houses with garrets on lower Paradise Street.

One, two, three, four, five,

Garrets in a row survive.

Six, seven, eight, nine, ten,

Build them up and use again.

Why did we let them rot?

Because no money we had got.

What did a builder do?

He made them safe and look like new.

The Christmas crib in the Market Place outside St. Michael's Parish Church.

CHRISTMAS SONG
(Tune: I had a little nut tree).

VERSE 1

We have a little manger in the Market Place,

Christmas bells are ringing, time to celebrate.

The shoppers now are gathering the Christmas lights to see,

And all for the sake of our lovely Christmas tree.

CHORUS

We surge into Mill Street, we crowd out Chestergate,

But all the people in the town cannot congregate.

St. Michael's in the springtime.

VERSE 2

When winter time is over and spring is in the air,

Flowers then are blooming, trees no longer bare.

St. Michael's church is witness to changing seasons all

And stands as a guardian behind its old stone wall.

CHORUS

We surge into Mill Street, we crowd out Chestergate,

But all the people in the town cannot congregate.

73

Sing a song of five pence,

A pocket full of silk,

Four and twenty kestrels

Drank a pint of milk.

When the milk was finished

The birds began to fly,

Then along came Charlie Tunnicliffe

With his artist's eye.

The staff were in the Town Hall

Counting lots of money,

The Mayor was in the parlour

Thinking it was funny —

That mayors no longer have to

Live in Macclesfield,

For since we were reorganised

The Borough's fate is sealed.

The new extension of the Town Hall
which now houses several
departments including that of
The Borough Treasurer.

The old Town Hall roof at one time was home to a family of kestrels.

The Festivals House
on Park Lane.

Jonty's sweet shop — liquorice and lime,

Had to close before its time.

Converted to an office block

Now Festivals make up its stock.

Nicholas Winterton, Tory M.P.
for Macclesfield having fun at
the Rossendale Centre's
summer fete in 1991.

We see him here, we see him there

Maxonians see him everywhere.

In news, on telly or just having fun,

That darn'd good-natured WINTERTON.

Nancy, Nancy, pretty and fancy,

How did your aviary grow?

With children's delight and feathers bright,

And chirpy birds all in a row.

The aviary in West Park.

The Two Hamlets — Early one Sunday morning under the verandah of West Park Museum.

To dream! perchance to sleep — ay, there's a thought;

For if we sleep what dreams may come,

When we have shuffled round this affluent town.

Yet we must pause and rest a spell.

Though destitution does make cowards of us all,

we'll bear the ills we have, than move elsewhere

for those we know not of.

Churchill Way — Rear of Market Hall and new extension to Cheshire Building Society offices.

MODERN MACCLESFIELD

Modern Macclesfield, a town up-dating yet still holding hands with the past.

Good new offices, from groups creating a responsible theme that will last.

Georgian edifice, now re-inspiring a new generation to see

Splendid workmanship, pride in rebuilding that will work in the next century.

Regency Period Mill, Chester Road roundabout.

Looking in the past means looking forward, for under the sun nothing's new.

Ancient architects have left their drawings as ruins which people can view.

Georgian travellers went forth inquiring which countries were best to explore.

Greek Acropolis and Roman columns set styles for each entrance and door.

Houses on Brown Street showing the Etruscan style
with flower motif over the front door.

Classic emphasis, looking quite modern that youth might accept as its own.

Simple curvature from the Etruscan, which helps conservation atone,

Here in Macclesfield two hundred years ago building went on at a pace.

Manufactories mimicking temples, inclined to the same form and grace.

Edwardian fireplace still reflecting the Georgian taste for Classical columns in interior decorating.

Suiting everyone, such formulations were adapted for large or small halls,

Each embellishment was rapidly copied for staircases, ceilings and walls.

Every frontispiece seemingly echoed the atmosphere captured in Rome,

Re-awakening cultural tastes which the young dilettantes brought home.

Egyptian monuments seen by Napoleon, that Nelson then claimed as his own.

Strange shaped obelisks making memorials suited to people wellknown.

Temple vestibules, built for Osiris and all other gods in the sands.

Giant porticos carried by sailing ships to satisfy English demands.

The original entrance to the Town Hall completed 1823.

Stone built colonnades under the desert moon, caused thoughts of romantic design.

Small town atmosphere and wealthy citizens saw all of these cultures combine.

Giving Macclesfield some sense of direction, a hotch potch of interesting views.

Unique refurbishment creating for modern times a picture nobody must lose.

OUR NEW LIBRARY

Hurrah, at last it's here! — our smart new library.

Complete with high tec. gear, the atmosphere's just right.

Does everyone approve? Oh no, on the contrary

Some antiquated regulars were soon put to flight.

For them the good old days were in the old premises,

Where reading room, though small, was crowded to the door.

Now there's so much space, they've lost their brand of privacy,

No door through which to hide and more people to ignore.

Old District Bank building extended and refurbished to become the new Public Library on Jordangate.

Though parking now has gone — there's toilet facilities,

And lots and lots of room for reference and advice.

A small sized public hall for those with abilities

To entertain with lectures, slides and other things concise.

More cases for display means that books on Local History

Are readily to hand, with much microfilm support,

And on the Ground Floor we find cookery to mystery,

Within the marble hall a lift for elderly transport.

There's screens for exhibitors just past the counter.

An Enquiry Desk where books can be ordered from elsewhere,

But sad to relate that so near is the town centre,

The profile of security keeps us all too well aware

Of those amongst the crowd whose ways are so unscrupulous,

They'll steal a book, disrupt and shout to conquer others' thoughts,

But also in our lives we find those meritorious

Who treasure books and notes, and give libraries great support.

A SIGN OF OLD AGE

Well hidden behind the goods of a utilitarian store

Lie the dark decaying trappings of a very fine old residence.

Belonging to a Georgian house, the burgess's front door

Was so formally designed to impress with stylish elegance.

Those who called and entered in would discover a spacious hall

With large rooms leading off both to the left and to the right.

Today, alas, through gross neglect, old age has taken toll,

And what remains to passers-by is a somewhat dismal sight.

A drawing of the doorway in Chestergate as it would have originally looked in the 18th century.

V.B.Smith 1995

Abandoned and forlorn its once majestic pretty face

Is lost in competition with selected things in bags.

Disfigured now and sadly scarred the door jambs seem disgraced

And what exists of beauty once, is now degraded as old rags.

What fortune to survive in spite of its poor state,

Yet showing still some character and skill of one who cared,

A worker in wrought iron, who found time to concentrate

And make a superb work of art for a world, now unprepared.

89

THE DOLLS HOUSE

When Daniel Defoe travelled through Derbyshire county,

The people soon told him of a giant, then dead,

Whose grave, on a mountain top, had kept them in bounty

As they related their 'fairy tales' whilst collecting their lead.

Supposing this giant had lived a while longer,

And had sought out a present to give to his child.

His strides into Cheshire would have echoed like thunder

As he leapt over the forest fragmented and wild.

Whilst he cast his eye far 'cross the country before him

He would see a small castle, which would make a good toy,

Or chapel with tower on a rock as in tales of Grimm,

But his child was a daughter and not a young boy.

He would certainly stop to pick up the silk mill,

And holding it tight in the palm of his hand,

Would whirl round the wheel, until slowing it stayed still

For it only would function at his finger's command.

As he sat on the Moss Rooms and made himself comfy,

With one foot near the Bollin to cool off his big toe,

His appearance dishevelled and looking quite scruffy,

He ate all the sheep off the hill, Shutlingsloe.

Then with one big 'burp', which caused a mini tornado,

He swung round his head and a house caught his eye,

It stood on the edge of some fields, with an orchard,

"This must be a doll's house", as he lifted it high.

The barns standing near went in different directions,

And the cattle were knocked off their feet in his haste

To snatch up the prize, which he knew the affections

Of his daughter would claim, from this country of waste.

Its size was just perfect with rooms large and airy,

Its symmetry made it a doll's house supreme.

The lovely carved stairway led up from the pantry

To an attic of considerable dimensions and clean.

The front door was stout and surrounded by stonework:

The architrave carved like two classical horns.

Each sashed window slid, up and down like a Turk

On a horse through a scrub land infested with thorns.

So carefully placing the toy on its corner,

He reached in his pocket, his kerchief to find,

To wrap up the present for taking back to his daughter,

But his pocket was empty and he cursed in his mind.

Charles Roe House, Chestergate
looking like the perfect doll's house.

Then he suddenly saw that he was surrounded

By town people, angry like bees from a hive;

And a shouting and screaming arose, which just sounded

Like wasps in the distance, but barely alive.

HE LAUGHED, the ground shook, and he looked down quite kindly,

For their bravery he liked, then he saw the Town Clerk

And whispered his wish, speaking low and so quietly

To keep them all calm, but his voice made them start.

The Town Clerk was adamant, "You'll not take our buildings",

"We'll weave you a kerchief instead as a gift",

"And one for your daughter, if you leave our belongings".

"With finest pure silk through our patterns we'll sift".

An agreement was made and the giant soon was happy,

But it took quite some time for the silk to be dyed.

Yet the presents, when finished, were so gorgeous and lovely,

That the giant, with his kerchiefs, quickly left satisfied.

Behind each fairy story, there's usually a moral,

And this one must prove that when a giant arrives,

Don't let him snatch buildings or effect a removal,

With appropriate concessions we keep control of our lives.

The old Waters Green was a very different scene from what

we are experiencing today,

A river flowing fast, joined by streams where horses cast their

long shadows at the ending of each day.

A footbridge made of wood and cattle chewing cud close to

cottages surrounding turf of green,

And higher up the hill, the goats soon ate their fill and came

ambling down to drink from out the stream.

When industry arrived she used up each flowing tide and

redirected water as she pleased.

Rivers grew more grim as pollution entered in and an

urbanised new landscape was conceived.

Water went from view, as the township grew and grew, and

the streets were laid like blankets to conceal.

Each delightful twist and turn became nobody's concern, till

underground the flooding soon was real.

Waters Green circa 1810. Today the Queen's Hotel occupies the
site of the group of buildings in the centre of the scene.

The landlord of the 'Queen's' saw his cellars full of streams,

as he struggled hard to save his barrelled beer.

His customers soon knew when they saw him serve wet

through — but he still survived his Licensing career.

The 'Waters' struggled on, knowing well something was

wrong, dreading storms and heavy rains around the town.

Had Bollin burst its banks there'd be sand bags piled and

planks, and helping folks to safety — not to drown.

People failed to recognise that some sluice gates in the 'Eyes'

were causing serious flooding in the 'Dams',

Till engineers arrived and finally contrived to settle all the

problems with some plans.

Yet water has its way; whilst a short while it will stay where

Man decrees and forces it along,

It's Nature's strength and power that wins the final hour.

How could we then have got it all so wrong?

So we have today a tarmaced traffic way, where people

hurry through or park their cars.

The noisy bustling scenes, of Edwardian dealers' dreams

from the markets and the fairs, have left their scars.

The fountain now is gone, the greenery and the throng,

except on Friday nights when take-aways

See some youngsters congregate, taking drugs and spilling

hate; let's hope with time it's just another phase.

A THOUGHT

Has Macclesfield got middle-age spread?

Watch out good town before you are dead,

For too much girth from affluent living

Ensures bad health that's unforgiving.

Keep fit and slim and watch your diet,

Control your mind, help stop the riot,

But most of all your soul maintain.

It's character from which we gain!

THE SAUCER

Isn't it strange how we commemorate

The important things that happen in our lives?

To make something part of a pattern on a plate,

Or any form of pottery — to survive?

We drink from mugs with names and dates of birth,

And pictures of our Royal Family.

Some with silly verse and quotations full of mirth

And even scenes of monuments and sea.

We're not to blame, we're brainwashed from the past,

When a potter drew in slip upon a vase.

Then came cobalt blue dipped in glaze to make it last,

With inscriptions on apothecaries' jars.

When prints first arrived it was easier to make

Sets of things which tell a story or look grand.

A large mansion house with its stately park and lake

On a soup tureen with serving spoon and stand.

A saucer made to commemorate the
founding of the Sunday School 1796,
transferred to Roe St. 1813.

Apart from small flowers and pretty scenes with birds,

The Georgians loved their graceful country views,

Victorian pomp liked commemoratives with words,

And saw Gothic towers amongst their soups and stews!

Yet, best of all, were the tea sets and their pot,

Such handy, useful objects to provide

For a fete or high tea or displayed on a whatnot,

As their patterns were more difficult to hide.

It seemed quite right to count up every year,

Then after multiples of ten or twenty five,

To have an excuse for a reminder to appear

In the hope that something special had survived.

Though cups soon break, many saucers still remain

And are good things for display without their tea.

Several black and white now in Macclesfield maintain

The Roe Street Sunday School's Centenary.

So come next year we shall celebrate again

What was "Instituted seventeen ninety six".

Our saucers, then antique, to the visitors will explain

That our Heritage Centre's built from more than bricks.

Picture: 8th May
1995 — White Swan,
Rodney Street.

V.E. DAY REMEMBERED

Small flags fluttering in the breeze —

A token memory.

Fifty years since Europe at peace,

Where now the enemy?

"A quiet walk behind St. Michael's Church on Sunday afternoon . . . to view the hills"...

View looking southeast from behind
the Town Hall and Parish Church.

A Ramble Through Macclesfield

If anyone should ask me, "What would you like to see

And who would you like to meet in Macclesfield's past?"

I would ask them to accompany me and walk through town

And round about, and help them feel the presence of what was.

A quiet walk behind St. Michael's church on Sunday afternoon

To overlook the valley and the river down below, to view the hills,

This is where it all began a thousand years ago or more,

The wooded hillsides overrun with rabbits, wolves and boar.

Then, when the first lord came and built his mill to grind his grain,

And used the trees from up the hill to build his manor house,

And brought a horse and cattle, sheep and pigs, his family, and his servants few,

Yes I would say, "I want to meet you all, to see your land, to know how it first began."

Then I would fly two hundred years within an hour,

The hunting in the forest, all the cattle, sheep and pigs would multiply.

The families also, coming here with power to sell their produce and to buy, some would stay,

But what would really matter most? Which personality would pave the way for others?

One person more than any one I would ask to meet.

Someone so important to this place, who felt its atmosphere,

Who knew instinctively what makes heats beat, and knowing

Dedicated ground for pilgrims' feet and others, so determined was she to mark her stay.

A princess from a foreign land, from Spain, a daughter of Castile,

And what strange turn of fate gave her the forest and the manor here?

And having gained, she also gained a crown to be the wife of Edward One, Queen Eleanor.

Her thoughts, concerns, good deeds, her saintly ways she hoped would settle here and grow.

But within the forest's boundaries so far and wide, lived boorish men,

Who hunted, drank and swore, and used their bows and arrows and their swords.

Some brawled and killed, and yet whilst Eleanor survived

She chose her servants well and one, a good and powerful man, kept peace.

Then I would want to meet this man of fame, Thomas of Macclesfield,

To ask from whence his family came, and why?

And moving on, to where the crenellated house was built half way up the hill,

Was this man John his kith and kin, or had someone usurped the family name?

I would demand to see the castle and explore the inner rooms and halls,

I would wander up the steep Wallgate. And how long would it take

To reach the chapel? I would hesitate to look inside,

Because two hundred years again had passed and there a funeral I espied.

But now the chapel does not stand alone, for next to it of stone

Another smaller chapel stands, built for a knight called Legh,

And yet another larger one, wherein its walls a priest taught school.

I see the priest; am I too late to take his hand?

And tell him just how well he had applied his talents to the Grammar School?

But hold, with master gone, the school moves on,

Behind the church where first our walk began.

Please let me step back to the chapel door and pay my last respects,

For there I see the mourners vigilant and holding candles large which flicker in the dark,

And altars with their shrines on which hang golden hearts.

How many decent, stalwart men have lain before Our Lady in this town?

In Tudor times, do I imagine all is quiet?

So little still remains of burgesses and properties and trading rights.

One man as mayor appears so many times and I must say,

"Mr. William Healey why are you so popular and why is there much decay?"

"My dear, have you not heard? Some fifty years ago a call to arms"

"Took many men to Flodden Field never to return."

"A generation gone, the town stood still, but yet the memory lingers on."

The chapel now has lost its Roman soul, but still it breathes,

For Catholic it remains, and will until tomorrow.

Neglected and forlorn, did Eleanor glide past and shed a tear

On pavings worn, where cattle, sheep and pigs go foraging?

And has the wool trade lost its old appeal? Or is there something else to do?

When did the silk arrive in town? I wish I knew.

But now we must move on to other parts for there awaits an aggravating time,

The Civil War arrives when Cavaliers and Roundheads muster to and fro; but who is foe?

The Colonel Legh of Adlington is captured in the strife,

And I shall want to know how the ordinary citizens in Macclesfield survive.

These people were a fascinating lot, a mixture thrown together by their trades.

The Quakers came — the Derby influence proved quite strong,

And then Dissenters found themselves their own dear plot to build upon,

And do you see today, their chapel still remains so neatly tucked away?

Jordangate was held by Church of England folks, at least until the 19th century approached,

And there's a door I really want to knock upon.

"Please Mr. Stafford may I stop and talk, or is your ghost too busy to respond?"

To you great man I want to say goodbye, and wipe away a tear and ask you, "Why?"

What of your neighbour, good hardworking Mr. Roe?

For long enough I sought him everywhere. How could

I have missed his talents and his works?

But now there is no need to stay and pass the time of day,

I know you well and in due course of time I promise I will others tell.

Listen hard, for on the wind you will hear the bagpipes coming near.

And look up at John Stafford's house where at the garret window he appears.

I will wave to reassure him all is well, but he will know

The rebels do not stand a chance, they think they do but they are wrong — Prince Edward

Stuart is gone!

At last the time has come for peace, at least at home though not abroad,

And industry will now increase in every way through water power and steam.

Please may I introduce myself to very special men, a considerable group of citizens?

And join the gathering at the Angel Inn and look for those I know by name and deeds?

There's Huxley, Glover, Robinson, Mr. Lankford and John Hale,

There's Hooley, Hulley, Sam Pearson, the Brocklehursts and Ryle,

A hundred more I ought to know for I've met so many names,

In pages kept in history books, parish registers and files,

And in the local library, Local History notes compiled.

The population's growing, we are being crowded out and money seems the order of the day.

There's Hawkins, Mills & Company, they have led the way, and opened up a bank on Jordangate.

These gentlemen, who came to town because of copper trading, Have issued penny tokens fine, with superb engraving,

But soon will leave, and in their place will come some more upgrading both their industry and homes along the way.

Now, on the outskirts of the town in fields, on greens and moors,

Comes one who is a conscience for them all, who speaks out boldly and endures.

"What good is wealth and commerce? Save your souls!"

"But Mr. Wesley with the money that we gain, we do good, give people parks and food".

The time machine is moving on quite fast, with Empire growing and prosperity to last

Another hundred years. Though silk eventually will fade away,

And yet it lingers on, for here the Brocklehursts come to purchase farms and land,

With civic calls to help the people understand. Please may I speak with them, one and all both young and old?

Especially Miss Marianne, whose interest in Egyptian things,

The relics of an unseen race, bewilders and attracts us all.

A face presented, set out fine, in cases carved to suit,

Within West Park's museum, built by one so resolute who undertook to travel many miles.

When in the twilight, as the setting sun departs the town,

This little corner lingers on, a place for peace and ponderings.

The busy Prestbury Road and hospital close by are shut out fast,

And here the mind can wander in the past, amongst the sand dunes of the Nile,

For Seb-en-mut is smiling such a smile that intrigues,

"Please tell us all your secret!" we implore.

Now let us leave the Fields of Town, where people ploughed and cattle grazed, and pass into the

Park.

For centuries this land was sown and oxen, sheep and piglets too were reared, and many

undertook

To feed their families and their friends. No revolution here.

When General Cholmondeley finally expired, his nephew sold this land to everyone who chose to

buy his own fine plot.

If we can beckon horse and carriage small, we'll drive away to Gawsworth Hall, a seat of power.

The Fittons reached their finest hour in Tudor times and now the Bard is annually recalled.

Whilst on the lawn we picnic and enjoy the entertainment and the wine,

A feast of pleasure, on and off the 'stage', do we encounter as we dine — the weather's fine.

Returning home we pass the grave of one who loved to laugh and sing, Lord Flame,

The jester who gave everyone a chance of happy, silly fun, and then passed on.

Please stop, I want to ask him "Were you really happy then or was it all a game?"

"Did you not love and in return want love from all around, and care?"

"I'm sorry I've no time to stay and wait reply, here comes the rain".

As down Park Lane we sweep along in style, Edwardians nod and Georgians wave,

Victorians condescend to stiffly smile as heavy window drapes black out their private lives.

So now today how does a modern world fit their designs?

Shall I pretend I've lost my way and knock on doors to really find the truth?

Or must I lead you all 'up town'? "Oh, no", you say, "we know the way",

"We've walked it many times before". But will you understand, can you explore alone?

And when you're bored, or drunk or high on drugs, what shallowness is there?

Just stand behind the Church in your despair — look to the hills — that's where it all began.

And feel the inspiration of the past, shake off your cares,

Help build a decent future that will last — for MACCLESFIELD.

*"Then, when the first lord came ... And used the
trees from up the hill to build his manor house"...*

Trees in South Park.

"Queen Eleanor. Her thoughts, concerns, good deeds, her saintly ways she hoped would settle here and grow".

Part of the stained glass window in the
Savage Chapel of the Parish Church.

"...wherein its walls a priest taught school".

The Savage Tower and Chapel.

"... the School moves on, Behind the church where first our walk began".

Part of the school

The end looking toward the church.

Adapted from a sketch (said to
be the only one in existence) of the
Old Grammar School on Bunker's Hill.

The south door of St. Michael's which is in the approximate position of the original entrance to the chapel.

"Please let me step back to the chapel door and pay my last respects"...

"And do you see today, their chapel still remains so neatly tucked away?"

On left the entrance through to the
King Edward St. Chapel, which is
situated out of sight behind the
Old Bank Building.

John Stafford. Original painting
by Joseph Wright of Derby.
Sadly only this poor copy is available.

*"Please Mr. Stafford may I stop and talk, or is
your ghost too busy to respond?"*

"What of your neighbour, good hardworking Mr. Roe?"

Charles Roe painted
by Joseph Wright of Derby, 1769.

"And join the gathering at the Angel Inn ..."

c.1940 On the left the old eighteenth-century
façade of the Angel Inn.

"There's Hawkins, Mills & Company, they have led the way, and opened up a bank on Jordangate."

Edward Hawkins, painting by
Sir Thomas Lawrence (1769 - 1830)
— the most famous portrait painter
of the period.

Front entrance to
Museum, West Park.

"A face presented, set out fine, in cases carved to suit,
Within West Park's Museum, ..."

"... We'll drive away to Gawsworth Hall ..."

Gawsworth Hall.

"... The grave of one who loved to laugh and sing,
Lord Flame,"

Grave, Maggoty's Wood, Gawsworth.

As down Park Lane we sweep along in style ..."

Former chapel at
the 'bottom end' of
Park Lane.

"Shall I pretend I've lost my way and knock on doors to really find the truth?"

Doors of houses on
Park Lane near
Brown Street.

*"Just stand behind the church in your despair –
look to the hills – that's where it all began"*

View from behind the Parish Church,
overlooking Sparrow Park.

Also of interest . . .

GOLDEN DAYS: A MACCLESFIELD LIFE – Paul Maybury *(£6.95)*

PORTRAIT OF MACCLESFIELD – Doug Pickford *(£6.95)*

MACCLESFIELD, SO WELL REMEMBERED – Doug Pickford *(£6.95)*

MACCLESFIELD, THOSE WERE THE DAYS – Doug Pickford *(£6.95)*

PORTRAIT OF WILMSLOW , HANDFORTH & ALDERLEY EDGE – Ron Lee *(£7.95)*

PORTRAIT OF STOCKPORT – John Creighton *(£6.95)*

PORTRAIT OF MANCHESTER – John Creighton *(£6.95)*

PORTRAIT OF WARRINGTON – Jen Darling *(£6.95)*

SHADOWS: A NORTHERN INVESTIGATION OF THE UNKNOWN – Steve Cliffe *(£7.95)*

DARK TALES OF OLD CHESHIRE – Angela Conway *(£6.95)*

CHESHIRE: ITS MAGIC & MYSTERY – Doug Pickford *(£7.95)*

MYTHS AND LEGENDS OF EAST CHESHIRE – Doug Pickford *(£5.95)*

SUPERNATURAL STOCKPORT – Martin Mills *(£5.95)*

Country Walking:

MOSTLY DOWNHILL IN THE PEAK DISTRICT – Clive Price *(£6.95) (two volumes, White Peak & Dark Peak)*

EAST CHESHIRE WALKS – Graham Beech *(£5.95)*

TEA SHOP WALKS IN CHESHIRE – Clive Price *(£6.95)*

TEA SHOP WALKS IN THE PEAK DISTRICT – Norman & June Buckley *(£6.95)*

WEST CHESHIRE WALKS – Jen Darling *(£5.95)*

RAMBLES AROUND MANCHESTER – Mike Cresswell *(£5.95)*

PEAKLAND RIVER VALLEY WALKS – Tony Stephens *(£6.95)*

Cycling . . .

OFF-BEAT CYCLING IN THE PEAK DISTRICT – Clive Smith *(£6.95)*

MORE OFF-BEAT CYCLING IN THE PEAK DISTRICT – Clive Smith *(£6.95)*

50 BEST CYCLE RIDES IN CHESHIRE – Graham Beech *(£7.95)*

CYCLING IN & AROUND MANCHESTER – Les Lumsdon *(£7.95)*

Sport . . .

RED FEVER: from Rochdale to Rio as 'United' supporters – Steve Donoghue *(£7.95)*

UNITED WE STOOD: the unofficial history of the Ferguson years – Richard Kurt *(£6.95)*

DESPATCHES FROM OLD TRAFFORD – Richard Kurt *(£6.95)*

MANCHESTER CITY: Moments to Remember – John Creighton *(£9.95)*

MANCHESTER CITY FOOTBALL CLUB: AN A-Z – Dean Hayes *(£6.95)*

GOLF COURSES OF CHESHIRE – Mark Rowlinson *(£9.95)*

- plus many more entertaining and educational books being regularly added to our list.
All of our books are available from your local bookshop. In case of difficulty, or to obtain our complete catalogue, please contact:

**Sigma Leisure, 1 South Oak Lane, Wilmslow, Cheshire SK9 6AR
Phone: 01625 – 531035   Fax: 01625 – 536800**

ACCESS and VISA orders welcome – call our friendly sales staff or use our 24 hour Answerphone service! Most orders are despatched on the day we receive your order – you could be enjoying our books in just a couple of days. Please add £2 p&p to all orders.